Organising Idea No. 2

A monograph published by the
EUROPEAN THERAPY STUDIES INSTITUTE

Psychotherapy, counselling
and the human givens

HG Publishing Ltd for the
European Therapy Studies Institute
Chalvington, East Sussex BN27 3TD, United Kingdom

Printed in Great Britain

ISBN 1 899398 95 3

Psychotherapy, counselling and the human givens

Joseph Griffin & Ivan Tyrrell

The words *therapy* and *therapist* come from the Greek term 'therapeia', which means treating and ministering to the sick – the art of healing. Therefore *anyone* who works to improve the health and well-being of another individual or group is acting as a therapist. This includes psychotherapists, counsellors, carers, social workers and complementary therapists as well as those working in orthodox medical settings such as doctors, nurses and psychiatrists. 'Therapist', consequently, is the only useful umbrella term that describes the function linking all people who are genuinely able to help others recover from, or adapt to, disease or distress.

We can see no useful distinction between the term psycho-therapist and counsellor. The only distinction we make concerns how effective someone is at lifting depression, reducing anxiety, detraumatising people, stopping addictive behaviour etc. What they call themselves, what qualifications they have, what trade association they belong to etc., is immaterial, so these terms are used interchangeably throughout this monograph.

We also use the terms client and patient interchangeably, although we are aware of the research that suggests most members of the public do not like to be thought of as 'clients' and prefer 'patient'.

Organising Ideas

"All scientific knowledge is a correlation of *what* is seen with the *way* that it is seen."

Henri Bortoft, *The Wholeness of Nature*

In all fields confusion flourishes, mistakes are made and harm is done when we forget that the *way* we look at phenomena is dependent on an active effort of imagination and thinking. We are not mechanical recording instruments looking out on a fixed world (although this is certainly the philosophy of science which is usually communicated by the way science is taught in schools, presented in popular books and revealed in television programmes). We *organise* what we see through what we believe we know.

When a field of study is confused about something, it usually needs a new organising idea.

An organising idea plays an active role in shaping our perception, thinking and research, and is always larger than earlier ideas because it has to explain the anomalies that previously caused confusion.

This paper, one of a series commissioned by the European Therapy Studies Institute, offers a new organising idea.

ETSI 2002

"The analysis of a situation is one thing, the prescription of the remedy, when indicated, is another.

"Diagnostic capacity does not prove therapeutic ability.

"In dealing with human conditions, the procedure almost always has to be specific, not generalised."

Idries Shah

Psychotherapy, counselling and the human givens

THE often confusing world of psychotherapy and counselling – which is only slowly emerging into the light of scientific enquiry – is under attack.[1,2] Periodically reports come out showing that neither does much good and both often actually do more harm than good.[3] There are also ongoing academic arguments within the profession, and confusion outside, as to the difference, if any, between counselling and psychotherapy and who should be considered qualified, and on what grounds, to practise. Rarely do counselling tutors demonstrate the techniques they espouse in front of students with real patients and there are no standardised assessment criteria for counsellors and psychotherapists across the different schools of therapy. Few courses even assess the students' effectiveness with real patients before qualifying them to practice.

Estimates vary but currently there are at least 400 different 'therapy' models on offer throughout the world[4] – which indicates the general lack of shared perceptions about how best to help people. In other words, generally, psychotherapy is still at a primitive level of development.

This situation is clearly chaotic and bewildering for all concerned including members of the general public seeking help and those sincerely trying to provide it. It also bothers neuroscientists, like Professor Ian Roberstson who said recently, "I am dismayed at how counselling and psychotherapy practice in many areas has become wilfully divorced from evidence and science to the extent of becoming self perpetuating cults in some cases. No one has the right to pick and choose a theory as a matter of personal preference and then offer it as a service to someone when there is a possibility that that service might do harm. We have to move towards evidence based practice and away from cults and ideologies."[5]

In an attempt to resolve this confusing state of affairs members of ETSI set about developing a new way of looking at psychotherapy which asked us all to look again at what we think we know. Many professionals found that the result of this effort brought a refreshing clarity of thought and vision to the field, enabling people to see more clearly what is of value in any particular therapy method – and what is not. It quickly became known as the 'human givens'[6] approach and was inspired by the simple idea that therapy *always* works best when it operates not from an emotionally frozen ideological standpoint, but from a real understanding of what it is to be a human being.

The human givens approach draws its power from observation, research, experience, the neurobiological and psychological sciences, as well as our collected heritage of wisdom gathered from many cultures down the ages. It says that, to be effective, a therapist has to be aware, not only of the basic physical and emotional needs programmed into us by our genes, but also of the nature of the resources endowed to us to get those needs met in the environment. These needs and resources together comprise the 'human givens' and are the way each of us fulfils our genetic potential. When needs are met well, they provide purpose, achievement and understanding and thus promote mental health; when used wrongly, they cause misery and mental illness.

Most people accept that, to feel valuable and fulfilled, our emotional needs have to be met. We can list some of the main ones, along with some of the resources, as follows:

Emotional needs include:

- Security – safe territory and the room to unfold well
- Sense of autonomy and control
- Being part of a wider community
- The need for attention (to give and receive it)
- Friendship, fun, love, intimacy
- Being emotionally connected to others
- A sense of status within social groupings
- A sense of achievement
- The need for meaning – being stretched.

The resources nature gave us include:

- The ability to develop complex long term memory
- Imagination which can allow us to focus our attention *away* from our emotions in order to problem solve more objectively
- The ability to understand the world through metaphor – complex pattern matching
- An observing self – that part of us that can step back, be more objective and recognise itself as a unique centre of awareness
- The ability to empathise and connect with others
- A rational mind to check out emotions
- A dreaming brain that preserves the integrity of our genetic inheritance every night by metaphorically defusing emotionally arousing introspections not acted out the previous day.

These needs and tools together are the human givens, nature's genetic endowment to us. They are handed down through the generations in our genes and, automatically (in undamaged people) seek their fulfilment in the environment.

It is the quality of the way those needs are met that determine the physical, mental and moral health of an individual.

Just as human givens are interconnected and interact with one another, allowing us to live together as many-faceted individuals, it seems that different therapy approaches also need to interact if they are to be capable of addressing the different elements of who and what we are. Yet, as each new therapy approach to dealing with human distress is launched upon the world, it immediately begins a process of entrenchment, digging itself into a rut by developing a systematic philosophy of therapy to be applied mechanically to every person with a problem.

All major therapies seemed wonderful to some people in their heyday. Perhaps the most valuable thing Sigmund Freud's psychoanalytical therapy did at the beginning of the 20th century, for example, was to highlight and draw the attention of the Western world to the ancient insight that many of our everyday behaviours are largely controlled by unconscious processes. However, the value of incorporating this simple but important truth into our culture was then largely undermined by Freud himself. Driven as he was by Messianic ambition and paranoia, and operating out of invented, unrealistic models of human functioning and psychology, based largely upon the mechanistic 19th century understanding of biology, he mounted a propaganda campaign for his bizarre ideas. Thus he effectively muddied the waters of psychiatry, psychotherapy and counselling for the remainder of the last century. The development of complex psychoanalytical theories (which were never scientifically tested by Freud or his followers, only asserted as true) was based, in Freud's case, on only six published case histories, all of which were disasters from the point of view of his patients.[7] The legacy of psychoanalysis and its offshoots is a disturbing story of misguided, often harmful, treatment.[8]

Behaviour therapy, which developed partly as a reaction to

the absurdities of psychoanalysis, also contained a profound insight. While others were still grappling with the 'deep unconscious', behaviourists discovered that changing behaviour was often able to help people resolve problems. They made use of the knowledge that there are innate pleasure circuits in the brain which can be stimulated by certain behaviours. When people were shown how to structure more desirable behaviours – behaviours more rewarding than their destructive ones – they found it easier to make healthy changes. And the reason it often worked was that, if people can get their physical and emotional needs met they will not be suffering from anxiety, anger, depression addictions and so on. When any counsellor clearly targets the elimination of behaviours that are stopping a person's needs being met, they are bound to have success. Encouraging depressed people to get more physically and socially active, for example, stimulates an increase in serotonin production and thus helps to lift clinical depression. That is powerful therapy.

Unfortunately, behaviourism in the way it was taught swelled into a total philosophy which would brook no dissenters. Students were told: *there is no such thing as consciousness, there is no such thing as mind. What you think has no effect upon you. You are your behaviour and nothing else.* Pure behaviourism became a gross distortion of what humanity is about. It undermined values and meaning in life and took away people's personal autonomy.[9]

We then had the growth of client centred therapy – active listening – developed by Carl Rogers. His idea was that, if you truly listen to somebody with a problem, and let them know that you *are* really listening, by feeding back your understanding of what their problem is, you are delivering very powerful therapy. Patients do need to have their story heard in a respectful, non judgemental atmosphere. Sometimes when a person is temporarily emotionally overloaded, just to have their story heard in a supportive way is all that is required for them to calm down, get a bigger perspective on their life situation and chart a way forward. Most people coming to therapy, however, need more than support. They have to borrow someone else's brain for a while to help them lower their emotional arousal and think clearly and learn so that they can move on. Their counselling may involve social skills training, learning anxiety or anger management skills, getting help with an addiction, or being detraumatised from terrible past experiences that are influencing their present behaviour. So, although active listening *is* an important component of therapy, it is usually only a small part. But, with person centred counselling, again the inevitable happened. Active listening expanded into a philosophy which said: *all anybody needs is for someone to really listen to them and a 'self-actualising principle' inside them will then manifest itself and sort all their problems out.*[10]

This is beautiful idealism but, as we have seen, painfully wrong. For example, you can listen to somebody with depression for ever and a day and they may still not come out of it, in fact they may become more deeply depressed. (This is why psychodynamic 'insight' therapy is contra-indicated for treating depression – the depressive trance state has to be broken, not deepened.[11]) It could well be that one of the main reasons for research findings showing that counselling is ineffective for helping people[12] is that counselling training is still largely based on this active listening/self-actualisation philosophy. Of course knowing how to listen is a vitally important skill, but much more is needed to effectively help people with emotional problems.

The more recent and somewhat more successful approach, cognitive therapy, is clearly going the same way. Cognitive therapy is based on the straightforward idea that, if we can get people to use their rational mind and question the evidence for their damaging negative belief systems, they can change. Helping people to make more realistic assessments of their life *is* powerfully effective, especially if they suffer from depression or anxiety. But in cognitive therapy we already see the same degenerative process at work. The original brilliant insight, which could be grasped at a single workshop, generated an enthusiastic following. But then pedantic people become involved and began writing complex books about it. Eventually ever more complex books about the complex books were written, littering psychology bookshelves, and people have now come to believe that several year's training is required to discover what cognitive therapy is all about before they can practise it on the public.[13]

This seems to happen with every school of therapy – psychodynamic, Rogerian, behavioural, biomedical, gestalt, cognitive etc. Many of them began with a useful insight but then became closed systems of thought unable to look at the totality of what it is to function as a human being. Cognitive therapy, for instance, focuses primarily on the rational aspect of the human mind as a means of lifting depression or anxiety. We could equally accurately say that problems are caused by a misuse of imagination and that a solution is to help people use their imagination more effectively.[14]

As therapies become complex, so they develop jargon that makes them incomprehensible to outsiders. As Hakim Jami said, commenting on this perennial tendency back in the 15th century: "If the scissors are not used daily on the beard, it will not be long before the beard, by its luxuriant growth, begins to think it's the head".

As a rule, when an approach starts getting really complex,

you can be certain it is going wrong – it is trying to make up for what it lacks by doing even more of the same. An organic integration of the insights contained in each school then becomes impossible. That is why the new human givens approach is so valuable – it helps therapists to see how all these elements interrelate.

People coming from a psychoanalytical perspective have said that the human givens approach only deals with symptoms, not the underlying problem. But research and experience does not support them. When time is spent digging up everything you can remember of what went wrong in your life, and exploring problematic past relationships in an effort to 'understand', it does not improve confidence or give you the skills to deal with life today. And yet such psychological archeology was the dominant approach in therapy for a long time. It still lingers on in some quarters and is still how psychotherapy is portrayed in the media and by those in the entertainment industry, who don't yet realise that Freud and Jung have little practical relevance to modern psychotherapeutic practice and may well come to be seen as having held it back from developing more quickly.

So what is effective therapy? Until the 1970s studies seemed to find that all therapies were roughly as good or bad as each other at solving human problems.[15] This was because, for the most part, therapists were rating their own effectiveness. More objective research has overturned that view. We now know that certain approaches are hugely effective in helping people and others much less so – some are even harmful. For example, when many hundreds of efficacy studies were looked at together, in a meta-analysis, brief, solution focused therapy was proved more effective for the treatment of anxiety disorders, depression, phobias, trauma and addictive behaviour than any long-term psychoanalytic style of therapy or drug treatments.[16, 17, 18]

What follows is an explanation of some of the most important human givens, which are now informing the work of today's most effective counsellors and psychotherapists.

The emotional mind and trance states

The first 'given' to look at is one that the whole human race crucially needs to understand – because misunderstanding of it is, ultimately, what causes the most suffering: from individual private misery to open warfare between nations. It is that high emotional arousal focuses and locks attention. This insight explains how the emotional part of our mind works and how it is connected up; and that, when the emotional mind is aroused, it can inhibit the higher levels of the brain, making us less than human. The process was memorably termed 'emotional hijacking' by psychologist Daniel Goleman. As he says in his book *Emotional Intelligence*, "In the dance of feeling and thought the emotional faculty guides our moment-to-moment decisions, working hand-in-hand with the rational mind, enabling – or disabling – thought itself. Likewise, the thinking brain plays an executive role in our emotions – except in those moments when emotions surge out of control and the emotional brain runs rampant."[19]

The emotional mind, which is highly active during dreaming and is what puts us into the dream trance state, also puts us into trance states when we are awake. A trance state is one in which we have only one focus. Think of anger, where we are so focused we can only see reality from one limited standpoint – one dimensionally. We become simple minded. Anger is a common, easily observed trance state and, whilst in it, we are as certain about the 'rightness' of the feelings as we are of the 'reality' of a dream. We all know that when we get very emotional we lack judgment, so any kind of over-emotionally aroused state, not just anger, makes us more 'stupid'. Strong

15

emotions lock our attention and thus prevent us having access to the bigger picture.

This is why policemen around the world have a jaundiced view of the intelligence of the general public. They so often have to deal with members of the public in crisis situations when they are emotionally aroused – shortly after accidents and at scenes of crime and violence. People talk 'stupid' on those occasions because they are emotional, and the daft things people say are often written down in police notebooks. For example, one policeman noted down the words of a distraught motorist, who had run over a woman pedestrian and had said to him: "She was dithering, officer! She was dithering all over the place, so I ran her over!"

Emotional arousal makes us stupid. The importance of this basic fact cannot be over-emphasised. Therapists, consultants and doctors need to always keep in mind that, when patients are emotionally aroused because of concerns about a diagnosis or worries about facing up to a crisis in their life, *they cannot process information accurately*. As a consequence they tend not to absorb information or insights that the doctor or therapist may be directing towards them. Indeed, GPs always need to be aware of this. Patients who come into their surgery are commonly emotionally aroused and so the advice or instructions they are given will often be misunderstood or go unheeded *unless the patients have actually been helped to calm down first*. This is especially so if a diagnosis with significant consequences is being given. That is why patients going to see a medical consultant are often advised to take somebody with them to take notes of what is said, or are given written instructions which they can take away and read when they have calmed down. The patient, in an emotionally driven trance state during the interview, will only focus on the threatening element in the diagnosis.

But emotional arousal – anxiety, anger, fear, greed, lust, awe, elation – although often a problem for us, is not inevitably limiting. Indeed, we need these strong emotions on *appropriate* occasions. Our survival depends on them. Without strong emotional arousal we couldn't defend ourselves from attack or run away from danger. And sexual arousal for procreation requires a strong emotional input. But, whenever emotional disorders occur, it is *inappropriate* strong emotions that cause the problem. And it is important to appreciate that, up to a certain level, anxiety *improves* performance and may help us find solutions. When it is not overwhelming us, a little anxiety helps us rise to the occasion.

The focused trance state is like a narrowed-down beam of light on a specific aspect of reality, and this focus is essential for doing anything well in life. A craftsman has to be able to turn off all distractions and focus attention exclusively on the task in hand. The same applies to tennis players, musicians, mechanics, cooks, scientists, therapists, etc. It applies in public speaking or when sitting an exam or acting. When we have the resources and skills we need, the trance state is under control and working *for* us, because the thinking part of the brain is involved.

Things go wrong, however, when a certain threshold is crossed and the emotional mind takes over completely. Our higher mental abilities are swamped by the rush of emotional hormones and the ability to look at reality multidimensionally is switched off.[20,21,22] We are then trapped in an emotional trance state that offers us only a primitive, one dimensional view of reality with no access to the skills we need to perform properly.

This happens to a lot of people when they get anxious. In their trance state they are saying, "Oh dear, I think I'm going to do badly here," or "I won't be able to remember any information when I get into the exam room," or "Oh my God, what'll happen if I fail?"

Learning the skill of unfocusing attention from these negative trances and refocusing it appropriately is the essence of living life skilfully. It is the ability we all try to access when we set out to achieve something. One psychologist termed it 'flow'— when you get into the right state of mind and things just happen beautifully for you.[23] Sportsmen have taken to using the term 'being in the zone' to describe this same state.

That we go easily into trance is a human given. Anything that focuses attention will do it. Moreover, there isn't only one right form of therapy for ensuring a trance state works for the client instead of against them. Cognitive therapy, hypnotherapy, use of humour, imagination or the 'observing self' can all be effective, when the timing and context are right. But many therapists and counsellors are still unaware that they are involved in manipulating trance states.

Hypnotic responsiveness

The trance state, then, is natural to us. New research on dreaming shows us how various methods of inducing trance mimic aspects of the rapid eye movement (REM) phase of sleep.[24] Swinging a watch before the eyes of subjects induces the rapid eye movements of the REM state. A version of this method has recently been revived in the EMDR (eye movement desensitisation and reprocessing) technique for detraumatising memories.[25] The stage hypnotist likes to induce hypnotic trance by activating the 'startle response'– giving a sudden shock such as jerking the subject's shoulder and shouting "SLEEP!" in their ear. Such a shock activates the electrical signals, scientifically termed ponto-geniculate occipital (PGO) spikes, which arise in, and progress through, the lower brainstem (pons), mid brain (lateral geniculate body) and higher brain (occipital cortex). It is the same startle response that helps trigger REM sleep.

Hypnotherapists and complementary therapists frequently use relaxation and guided imagery, which duplicate the normal sleep induction patterns, to induce trance. Stage I sleep is very similar to REM sleep in the way thought is processed.[26] The hypnotist merely replaces the dream script with his own hypnotic patter and so activates the 'reality simulator' that is the REM state.[27]

Hypnotic ability is therefore one of the human givens and has enormous potential for mind/body healing. All forms of psychotherapies, and indeed many of the touch therapies, directly or indirectly trigger off hypnotic states in patients and clients, even if the therapists are unaware that this is what they are doing.[28] A wider awareness of the hypnotic process and its potential would obviously make therapy safer and more effective.

The role of the imagination

Imagination is another human given that works both for and against us. Very many of our problems are self generated through the misuse of our imagination and nowhere is this more true than in anxiety disorders and depression.[29] For instance, when people feel panic symptoms, they may start to imagine they are going mad or having a heart attack which further aggravates the panic. Agoraphobia usually develops as a result of associating a panic attack with a particular location. Imagination then starts to make misconnections with other locations and often succeeds in triggering off panic attacks in those locations as well, eventually leading to the person being unable to even leave their house.

The converse of this is that, if we learn to use the imagination constructively, we can disempower the negative states of mind.[30] One of the ways this can be done is through helping the client into their observing self (see below).

Memory involves imagination. When we remember something we are recreating a story about our past in the present. We retell the stories about what happened to us in the light that we want to portray events, according to what seems relevant now. We add and subtract detail, put in humour, pathos, excitement, romance, guilt or blame. Memories can never be an exact reproduction of what happened which is why they are notoriously capricious, even without any conscious elaboration. One barrister told us of a murder case in which 11 witnesses in a pub all saw a man stab another patron. They all said the attacker was wearing a hat, they all emphatically and honestly described it – but each differently from the others, and not one of them described it correctly.

The observing self

The concept of the 'observing self' comes from Eastern psychology where it was developed over many millennia.[31] It is only now being incorporated into Western psychology and an understanding of it is highly useful in dealing with post-traumatic stress, phobias, addictions, depression and anxiety states.

The observing self is a more fundamental part of us than even our thinking and feeling. It is our awareness and everything else feeds into it. A person could lose arms, legs, sight, hearing and the ability to think well, yet still exist – still have that sense of being a centre of the experience of reality: "I am"; "I am aware". In other words, the observing self supersedes thought, feeling and action *because it experiences these functions*. No matter what takes place, no matter what we experience, nothing is as central as the self that observes.

The observing self is incapable of being objectified. In the words of Dr Arthur Deikman: "Whatever you can notice or conceptualise is already an object of awareness, not awareness itself. Unlike every other aspect of experience – thoughts, emotions, desires and functions – the observing self can be known but not located, known but not 'seen'."

When people are trapped in depression, addictive behaviour, post traumatic stress, phobias or other anxiety disorders, they can be helped by being pulled back out of such trance states into their observing self. Then they can see the wider reality and refocus their attention in a way that's helpful and thera-peutic. There are many ways of snapping people out of their negative trance state and into their observing self. In narrative therapy[32], VK dissociation[33], guided imagery, etc, therapists use such methods to separate the core identity of a person from their problem. One such method was used with enormous power by American therapist David Epston, working with a 15 year old girl close to death from anorexia. You can see clearly from this vivid description by Bill O'Hanlon how Epston's style of questioning – talking about anorexia as if it were outside of her – eventually drove the dying girl back up into her observing self and began her recovery.

Rhiannon was a 15 year old girl who was close to dying from anorexia. Accompanied by her cousin and her cousin's boyfriend, she was a skeleton lost in a large sweater, trying to make herself invisible, curling her arms around herself and slumping down in her chair. Smiling faintly in response to David's persistent questions, she insisted she felt fine and had lots of energy. David, carried away by his intense interest in her answers, could barely contain himself. He squirmed in his chair, leaned toward the girl and asked her question after question: "Can I just ask you why you think it is that Anorexia tricks people into going to their deaths thinking they're feeling fine? What purpose would it have, getting you to go to your death smiling?"

Rhiannon still would not engage. Slumped in her chair she kept saying she felt fine. Rhiannon had recently been discharged from a hospital after losing 25 pounds in three weeks, and a physician was monitoring her condition three times a day. She was literally on the brink of death. At home she had been lying in a foetal position and screaming until her exhausted parents took her over to her older cousin's house.

As I watched the tape, I thought that even I, psychotic optimist that I am, would have given up on engaging Rhiannon and would have focused my interventions on the cousin and her boyfriend instead. But David seemed to be even more psychotically optimistic than I am. He persisted: "Okay, okay, okay. If that's how you're feeling, how's it fooling you? Most people, when they're near death, know they're being murdered, right? How's Anorexia doing this to you? Because if it's making you feel good or telling you you're feeling good, then I'd like for you to ask this question of yourself: "Why does it say to you you're feeling good? Why would it do this? Why does it want to murder you? Why doesn't it want you to protest? Why doesn't it want you to resist?"

Then, suddenly and inexplicably, Rhiannon responded. Anorexia, she said, fooled her by telling her she was fat when she was thin. "Is it telling you that right now?" David asked. "No," Rhiannon said. "I am too thin." She sat up in her chair.

David asked her how she knew that and she replied that people who love her told her that she is too thin. "Do you think Anorexia loves you?" he asked her. "No," she said. "It's killing me."

Her voice grew stronger. Her body language changed. In response to David's continual stream of questions, she began to make plans for standing up to Anorexia and not letting it fool her into starving herself any more. David enlarged the new doorway, asking her how, in the past, she had shown herself to be the kind of person who could stand up to something like Anorexia. By the end of the session, nobody in the room was talking about her hospitalisation any more. David, Rhiannon, the cousin and her boyfriend all looked hopeful and certain. Rhiannon had become an ally in treatment rather than a reluctant bystander.[34]

The search for meaning

Again it's part of being human – a given – to search for meaning. We all have to tell ourselves a story about what our life is about. Why did that happen to me? What is the meaning of my life? The innate urge to give meaning to what happens to us leads people to explain their problems in a variety of subjective ways: "It happens because I'm a loser." "It's hereditary; my mother had the same problem." "I have no will power." "It's because I'm unattractive." "Life's a bitch and then you die." "It's God's will." "I'm a Capricorn."

The search for meaning is a powerful therapeutic tool. There are a huge number of choices we can make on the journey through life. Some directions enrich and liberate us. Others are dead ends. If people arrive at a state where they feel life is meaningless or that they are useless human beings, then they need help from the therapist so that the barriers that stop them perceiving meaning can be broken down, leaving the client free to find it.[35]

The need for control

We all need to feel a measure of control over our life. Anxiety disorders often begin when a person feels control is slipping away and they become afraid that they are powerless to stop terrible things happening.[36] A fundamental principle when dealing with anxiety disorders is to help give a person back a sense of control over their reality. In the case of panic attacks, for example, this would be a sense of control over their physiology. Control, however, does not have to be absolute to be positive for mental health. It has been found that people who survived torture best were those who had a cast of mind that enabled them to retain a modicum of control over what was happening to them, even to the limited degree of counting to 10 before screaming or before passing out.[37]

When we look at what generates anxiety problems in our society, the one thing that stands out is the increasing rate of change in the world around us. Our biology has not changed for tens of thousands of years, but the changes we have made in our environment and the ways in which we now live have been dramatic. So the problem is that our ability to create always leaps ahead of our ability to adapt, and we are forever locked into a cycle of adapting to unprecedented situations.[38]

Also, if there are too many changes in our lives, such as the death of a loved one, taking on a new and demanding job, or moving to a new town or country, our ability to adapt may be taxed to the limit and we may become ill.

The more experiences we have in our lives of not having control, the more important it is to find those small areas we *can* control. It is often part of our job as therapists to help people do that. To function well, of course, everyone has to learn to live with the inevitable larger uncertainties in life and be able to tolerate ambiguity. Fortunately, as we learn more about the brain, we find that it has an ability to adapt to even the most trying of circumstances.[39]

Differences between male and female thinking

Human beings often seem to be in a state of continual fascination and exasperation with members of the opposite sex.[40] Sexual differences are endlessly explored, yet their implications are little thought out, probably because of the emotional arousal the implications engender. Differences include the language patterns and communication styles that men and women typically use, and differences in emotional response styles between men and women. Women are typically more emotionally sensitive and more aware of the nuances of their emotional feelings whilst men tend to direct more of their attention towards problem solving.[41] These two different response biases tend to be sex specific, but also complement each other and so help the human species be more adaptable.

Differences between the sexes appear at a young age. For example, boys are typically greater risk takers than girls, which leads to approximately four times more fatal accidents involving boys than girls.[42] It is also normal for boys to have shorter attention spans and be 'hyperactive' a lot of the time.

This tendency for risk taking and sensation seeking means that boys need more stimulation in order to focus and structure the way they give attention. This, of course, has an impact on the education styles that boys and girls respond to best. Typically girls make tremendous strides within the educational system when it is cooperatively based and they are subject to appraisal by continuous assessment. Boys need discipline and a more structured and stimulating approach before they can focus and work well. They tend to flourish in the high risk, competitive assessment style of exam systems. The statistic that up to 10 per cent of all boys are diagnosed as having attention deficit hyperactivity disorder (ADHD), an extreme form of the need for greater stimulation to focus attention, clearly shows how boys' attention needs are failing to be addressed by current educational practices.[43]

We do have natural instincts which require an appropriate environment for their normal development. Small boys, for example, need wild parks to roam in, trees to climb and the freedom to take risks, have adventures and rough and tumble games. Failure to find such places for them has consequences, as seen in the rise of ADHD which is predominantly a male problem and increasingly treated with the drug Ritalin. (Up to ten times more boys than girls are diagnosed with ADHD.)

Another natural instinct children have is to develop conversational relationships with adults. We now know that the large number (about 60%) of adults report social phobic responses and we now know that one of the major causal factors for this is insufficient conversation with adults when they were children. (The ubiquitous presence of TV sets in virtually every home, even the poorest, may be one of the causes of the rise in social phobias.)

When we fail to recognise that we have animal instincts that need to express themselves, it results, in our urban world, in unnatural environments for our children, particularly boys, which distorts the expression of their instincts and can lead to pathological behaviour. We should never forget that Nature produces variety to ensure the continuing survival of the species through adaptability. Our survival depends on a variety of personality types which means we need the quiet, studious, introspective child *and* the boisterous, extroverted, rebellious, hyperactive child.

It isn't just a small number of children who are disadvantaged by current child management/teaching styles. The increasing diagnosis of ADHD will increasingly pathologise more and more child behaviour, and we can expect the overall performance of male children to suffer if the environment continues to develop in a way that doesn't suit the expression of children's instinctive behaviour.

These mind/body sex differences extend even to different dietary needs. Men, for example, have a greater need for protein than women and are much less attracted to – and less well served by – a low meat diet.[44]

If, in this age of striving for equality between the sexes, we try to deny or defy these differences, we are actually losing information and knowledge and will ultimately be less able to meet the needs of either.

The need for attention

It has emerged only in the last 30 years that everyone needs attention.[45] Babies who don't get enough attention suffer terribly as a result. Oddly enough an experiment that proved this dates back to the 13th century, when Emperor Frederick II, ruler of Germany and Sicily, wanted to know whether babies, left to themselves, would speak the language of their parents or an 'original' language. He arranged for a number of babies to be brought up in absolute solitude. They were fed and kept clean but their caretakers were ordered not to talk or signal to them in any way nor show any signs of affection. But the experiment failed because all the children died – starved of attention.[46]

We need to understand that all human interactions have an attention interchange (giving, receiving, exchanging) element in them. The need for attention is an appetite that has to be satisfied. When we don't recognise this we become inefficient and have less capacity to plan and direct our own behaviour and make wrong emotional and intellectual connections. We should always remember that we can get by on a lot less attention than we crave.

Unless health professionals know this, it can distort their relationships with clients and they end up needing their clients as much as their clients need them. We need to be clear that, if a therapist *needs* clients in this way, then he/she is corruptly using them. Furthermore, therapists can end up damaged by their clients. This is because, when we interact with a client, *we* also go into a state of focused attention where we absorb information less critically than usual. Without being aware it's happening it's easy to absorb our client's misery, sense of hopelessness, negative views or even their whole value system. Over a period of time this can lead to burnout in the therapist and feelings of depression and alienation from their work.

The only natural corrector to this is for therapists to:

a) be aware of the process, which helps prevent being drawn into the client's world;

b) take corrective action by mixing with people who don't have such problems. In other words, get your attention needs met by having a sufficiently healthy social life outside of doing therapy.

The propensity for addiction

The human givens approach recognises that a propensity for addiction is intrinsic to human nature. This is because humans are attracted to altered states of consciousness. The brain naturally produces chemicals which alter our mood. When we are involved in a meaningful, absorbing and satisfying activity, for example, our mood is enhanced – we feel good. Humans are easily drawn to substance abuse and risk addiction because chemical substances exist which mimic that good feeling. If the substance abuse becomes compulsive an addictive trance starts to dominate the user's body chemistry, behaviour and outlook, setting them on a risky, degenerative spiral, seriously interfering with their natural or potential development. Robbed of the motivation for positive action, addiction is the result.

In fact any activity that alters our mood in a pleasurable

way has the potential to become addictive. We, in effect, become addicted to the manipulation of our own bio-chemistry. Common examples of this can be seen in addiction to gambling, pornography, sex chat lines, computer games, jogging and numerous other activities.

The risk of developing an addiction increases to the extent that our essential needs are not being met, whether this arises from environmental factors, lack of social skills or psychological damage. The probability of staying out of an addiction very much depends on how successful we become at getting our needs met. (Remember, needs are not the same as wants. Wants are manifestations of greed.)

Understanding these processes makes possible brief therapeutic interventions that can help many addicts rapidly regain control over their lives.

Flow

As we have seen (page 17) one of the most interesting abilities we have is to move into what some psychologists have come to call the state of 'flow'. This is the opposite of selfish addiction. It is essentially selfless.

A state of flow occurs when we switch our attention away from ourselves and become totally absorbed in some activity *for its own sake*. In such a state of consciousness we perform at our best, whether in our work, sport, art, craft, hobby, selfless service to others, or our intimate relationships. After we have experienced such a state of flow we usually feel our life to be more blissful and full of meaning. Csikszentmihalyi connects this directly to our longing for 'happiness':

"Happiness is not something that happens. It is not the result of good fortune or random chance. It is not something that money can buy or power command. It does not depend on outside events but, rather, on how we interpret them.

Happiness is in fact a condition that must be prepared for, cultivated, and defended privately by each person. People who learn to control inner experience will be able to determine the quality of their lives, which is as close as any of us get to happiness."[47] Burnout is not an issue for people who experience some measure of flow in their work.

We can see here that all the human givens are starting to interconnect.

Attention connects with meaning.

Meaning connects with flow.

Flow occurs when we are being 'stretched', pushing ourselves to the limit, and involved with something bigger than ourselves – this is how we remain mentally healthy. [48]

The need for community

One of the unfortunate trends of the 1970s and 1980s in Britain was the propagation of a philosophy that community does not exist. It was famously promoted by former prime minister Margaret Thatcher, who declared that "there is no such thing as society". According to this belief, we are just a collection of individuals involved in a race for the survival of the fittest. We can now see that putting that philosophy into practice, and ignoring the human need for a sense of society around us, did tremendous damage to the infrastructure of Britain.

We all need to connect with other people to stay emotionally well. Recent research shows that those who are most psycho-logically healthy are those who make a contribution to society, giving more than they are taking.[49] Such people don't just focus on their own needs. They also actively focus outwards and involve themselves in the wider community, be it the parent/teacher association, local youth club, church, a charity or some global concern. When we help others we are actually helping ourselves as well – improving physical health and strengthening our immune systems.[50]

This need to connect with other people to stay emotionally healthy is connected to the need for attention – giving and receiving it. The interchange of attention is nature's mechanism for enabling us to stabilise our consciousness in tune with that of our family and the 'tribe' or culture to which we belong. It also enables us to absorb uncritically the role models, morals, habits and culture of our tribe so that we can maintain our place as a member of it. This was a very necessary evolutionary development for our survival as a social animal.

The downside of this necessary mechanism is that each culture is relative, omitting or distorting certain value systems. This relativity is clearly seen when we look back over history at past cultures – the values of an ancient Roman were not the same as those of a Chinese emperor of the Han dynasty, or a South Sea islander before the coming of Europeans – but it is equally applicable today. And not only between countries, religions and races. The values and culture of a London lawyer are not the same as those of a London taxi driver, Northumberland hill farmer, Welsh businessman, Scottish actress or motorway maintenance worker from the Midlands. Although we each inhabit a primary tribe in our own country we are members of many other tribes, each with its own jargon, rituals and beliefs. The fact that we live like this, tribe piling on top of tribe, loosely coexisting but often incomprehending the reality of other tribes, creates many opportunities for misunderstanding and conflict, and suggests that the need for greater adaptability is becoming ever more critical in a world where technology is forcing us to become one global village. Where once whole civilisations could exist without being aware of one another, now each nation and tribe impinges increasingly more intrusively on the rest, putting ever greater demands on our collective tolerance and understanding.

There is an additional difficulty with the process of uncritically incorporating models of reality from our immediate family or tribe. If the family or tribe is dysfunctional, people need – but do not necessarily get – help to adjust their models of reality to make them less disruptive to the larger community. Dysfunctional families cause chaos all around them just as dysfunctional countries do. Indeed, if we are to continue our evolution as human beings we all need, at some point in our development, to stand back and critically evaluate such models to see whether or not their social values and religious, moral or political views accurately reflect the wider reality – life as we know it today. Failure to do so may result in our extinction in the not too distant future.

The mind/body connection

In the last twenty years it has become more apparent to scientific enquiry that the healing response is a rich system of mind/body communication. If the body is starved it can disturb the mind; if the mind is starved it can disturb the body. It is a two way street.[51, 52]

We now know, for example, that anxiety compromises the immune system to the point that it can speed the development of cancer; increase vulnerability to viral infections; exacerbate plaque formation leading to atherosclerosis and blood clotting, which in turn may lead to myocardial infarction; accelerate the onset of Type I diabetes and the course of Type II diabetes; and worsen or trigger an asthma attack. Stress can also lead to ulceration of the gastro-intestinal tract, triggering symptoms in ulcerative colitis and inflammatory bowel disease. The nervous system is subject to 'wear and tear' as a result of stressful experiences and even the brain itself is susceptible to the long term effects of sustained stress, including damage to the hippocampus, and therefore to memory.[53]

The psychological/brain involvement in health, we now

know, goes far beyond the scientific ideas of even a few years ago. In one massive study those in objectively poor health who rated their health as good had a higher chance of survival than those in objectively good health who rated their own health as poor.[54] It is now clear that what we believe about ourselves plays a part in allowing us to conquer pain, recover from disease and even survive against the odds, and it may well change our susceptibility to illness. This is why observation and listening is so important for therapists. One needs to understand the belief system of clients in order to help them in the most effective way.

The need for metaphor and dreams

Metaphorical communication is an intrinsic part of the way human beings understand and communicate experience. Metaphorical expression always occurs in dreams and is far more widespread in our waking lives than we have probably realised.[55] It is a human given important for therapists to understand because, just as we have the potential to identify appropriate metaphors, we may also make inappropriate matches between two patterns. A great many mental problems may be caused by these thinking processes going awry.[56]

To understand the role of metaphor fully, we first have to understand the role of dreams.

The dreaming brain

David Foulkes, a pioneer in scientific dream research, wrote that dreaming was "one of the core problems of cognitive psychology ... so central to the study of the mind that its resolution can help to reveal the fundamental structures of human thought."[57]

He was right. What's more, recently developed theories about why we dream have the ability to transform the effectiveness of psychotherapy.

In 1953 Aserinsky and Kleitman noticed that people, while asleep, exhibit periods of rapid eye movements, which quickly became known as REM sleep. They found that REM sleep occurs about every ninety minutes during sleep and occupies a total sleep time of between one and a half to two hours a night. During that time there is an inhibition of antigravity muscles (termed tonic immobility), so we are in a state of paralysis. Clearly something important is going on. When Nature makes us vulnerable, as it does when we are paralysed in REM sleep, the payoff must be considerable. The payoff, it was quickly realised, is dreaming. When subjects were awakened from REM sleep, they recalled a dream on about 80 per cent of occasions. Subjects awakened from non REM sleep recalled dreams on only 7 per cent of occasions, and these tended to be dream fragments, not whole dream scenarios.[58]

Other scientists soon discovered that REM sleep is a characteristic of almost all mammalian species – even birds show a little.

Moreover, REM sleep is predominant in the foetus during the last trimester of pregnancy when the foetus spends up to eighty per cent of sleep time in REM sleep. This declines to sixty-seven per cent at birth, declines further to approximately twenty-five per cent later in childhood and stays at approximately this level until old age, when it declines again. The amount of REM sleep at birth is directly related to the maturity of the animal. Those species born with their brains and physical abilities well developed show little REM sleep. In contrast, species who are born very immature show high levels of REM sleep. A species such as the guinea pig, which is well developed at birth, shows only about fifteen per cent REM sleep, whereas the rat, which is born blind and immobile, shows over ninety-five per cent REM sleep. The rat quickly matures and, within one month, REM sleep has declined to thirty per cent of total sleep time. Any comprehensive theory of REM sleep must be able to explain not only REM sleep in adulthood but also its preponderance during gestation and early childhood.

Another major breakthrough came when Michel Jouvet[59] surgically removed from cats the part of the brain that controls the body paralysis of REM sleep. The cats then seemed to act out their dreams – going through their instinctive behavioural repertoire: hunting, fighting, grooming, drinking, mating etc.

Jouvet went on to propose that the function of REM sleep is to programme instinctive behaviour.[60] This was born out when research demonstrated that young babies first show smiling, grimacing and other behaviours in REM sleep. Animals, before they are born, also exhibit instinctive behaviour in REM sleep, for example, 'breathing', even when there is no air in the womb.

New knowledge indicates that this is a metaphorical process. The programme, or template, for an instinctive behaviour has to be in analogical form because a mammal has to be able to adapt to variation and changes in the environment, and the demands of circumstances. A baby, for example, will seek out and suck on anything that resembles a nipple because no two nipples are exactly alike. It will also respond to a face-like shape because it cannot possibly know in advance the exact shape or colour of its mother's face. And children appear to have a template to learn a language but it has to match the patterns found in the environment into which it is born. So a baby born in England can be moved to Japan where it learns Japanese instead of English as its first language and it does so just as easily as it would have learnt English had it stayed in England.

If REM sleep is connected with the laying down of instinctive templates, what is its role when we dream?

The first theory to answer this puzzle, and integrate the apparently diverse biological, psychological, genetic and phylogenetic data, was published in 1997 (see *The Origin of Dreams: why we evolved to dream,* by Joseph Griffin). We believe it has provided a major new insight into how we think and the special function of analogical and metaphorical thought in human affairs. Professor Michel Jouvet himself described it as, "the bridge between neurophysiology and psychology."

The theory explains how dreaming is Nature's way of dealing with emotionally arousing introspections that haven't been acted upon when awake. In our dreaming at night, these introspections are acted out in metaphorical scenarios which deactivate the emotional arousal 'trapped' in the autonomic nervous system, thus freeing up brain activity for other concerns the next day.

The analogical theory of dreams can be summed up in three points:

- Dreams are metaphorical translations of waking introspections.

- But it is only introspections that caused emotional arousal which was not acted upon that become dreams.

- Dreams deactivate the emotional arousal which frees the brain to respond afresh to each new day.

Psychotherapists, as well as sleep and dream researchers, have shown interest in the book partly because of the practical use to which the discoveries can be put. A psychiatric nurse, for example, was working with a team helping refugees from Bosnia who had come to England. One man was suffering terrible nightmares about hand grenades going off in his mouth. It was known he had witnessed dreadful scenes of atrocity in Bosnia and the psychiatrist on the team was preparing to treat him for post traumatic stress syndrome. The nurse said: "Before we do that, let's ask him if there is anything bothering him here and now, in this country." They did so. It turned out that he was very worried that, because his English was not good, he might at any moment say something to upset the British authorities and as a consequence be sent back with his family to Bosnia. The hand grenades in his mouth were a metaphor for his worries about what he might say. He recognised the pattern in the dream immediately and, when he was assured that he would not be sent back, whatever he said, his nightmares stopped. (Repetitive dreams and nightmares are the result of persisting circumstances causing the arousal – a troubling situation that hasn't been resolved. Being economical, the brain, once it has a metaphor, will use it over and over again.)

The new insights into dreaming enable us also to see why it is that more and more children are coming to therapists with nightmares, symptoms of stress and even post traumatic stress disorder. We are finding that these are caused by the violent images they have seen on TV or on videos.[61] Adults are not immune to this either. We now find that a significant portion of the dreams of the average adult is given over to the deactivating emotional arousals caused by watching television. This is not an innocuous process. The continual activation by television programmes of the startle response in viewers not only means that we are having emotionally arousing introspections that need to be deactivated in dreams, and that part of our conscious capacity is being used up by it, but also that we are becoming desensitized to what might trigger off that startle response in other circumstances. This inevitably creates a need for ever more gross stimuli to trigger off the same level of arousal.[62] People who complain about the continual debasement of entertainment are usually told by people with vested interests in the entertainment industry that the programme makers are just satisfying public demand. It's true. They are. *But the demand is created by the programmes themselves and the effect they have on our mental biology.*

This has a grave but generally unrecognised consequence. Not only are television and film companies under pressure to produce ever more gross stimuli (programmes) in order to keep the emotional arousal going but, as we have seen, that same emotional arousal makes us generally more stupid by decreasing our ability to perceive reality objectively.

Just one such example of mounting stupidity associated with emotional arousal is the increasing confusion in our society in recent times between the use of pornographic, violent imagery and art. Since ancient times art has been recognised as that capacity to create artefacts or events which speak to us about universal patterns of such a subtlety that they are not readily understandable by the conscious mind. But there have arisen this century 'artists' who declare that the purpose of art is to shock. Hyper-emotional arousal, however, does not favour the development of discrimination and subtlety and is the opposite of what art evolved for (to express metaphorically the otherwise inexpressible). Clearly the confusion between emotion and significance narrows our options and diminishes our culture. Some supporters of crude, emotionally extreme popular entertainment say it is what the public wants. But this ignores the fact that, when emotions are stimulated by a drama of *any* kind, attention is locked until the pattern is run out. And this is hard to resist. The 'public' is not a free agent in such circumstances.

Metaphor in therapy

Metaphor is part of everyday language and experience, even for the simplest things. It is through metaphor that we communicate because the naked truth cannot be spoken. The nearest we can get to truth is by clothing it in metaphor. Thus we are forced by the nature of things to describe anything at all by beginning, "It's like..." This is so from the simplest examples, such as describing a new taste experience, right up to the complex, profound, multilayered meanings projected through teaching stories.

Creative insight is usually the result of taking a metaphor from one area of reality and seeing how it helps us make sense of another. So creativity, too, always uses metaphorical processes. It's how we discover new theories, develop our technology and express ourselves through the arts. Mathematicians also work by metaphor, building a symbolical model of an aspect of reality and then, by exploring the implications or the connections within that symbolical model, hoping to track or observe a similar pattern in nature.

At our highest creative level we use metaphor usefully and with great success. And when people are dealing adequately with life's ups and downs they are drawing on appropriate metaphors to steer their way through. Consequently, they don't have emotional problems. When people develop emotional problems, however, it is *always* because they are drawing on *inappropriate* metaphors. The problems arise because the person is distorting the current reality by the way they are interpreting the current situation based upon past learning patterns.

The dreaming process can be seen as tapping into the brain's very own virtual reality simulator which has a multitude of functions.[63] It can take partially described, non-sensory analogues of an experience, which is our instinctive knowledge programmed into us before we are born, and search the environment for something that corresponds to that pattern. That process continues throughout our life and we tap into it directly whenever we make emotional learnings. Our emotions are our instincts, so we are pulled into the brain's reality simulator when we learn things from an emotional basis. The new learnings in turn act like new instinctive templates, and we are forever scanning the environment for their metaphoric representations in the world.

Now, when those metaphorical templates are appropriate to our environment, there is no problem – they work beautifully. The map, so to speak, is accurate. But when the emotional templates do not match sufficiently well with the person's present reality, they have a problem.

The recognition that patients may have an inaccurate map of reality and that they can be helped to develop a more accurate one gives enormous scope to psychotherapists. It is an approach in great contrast to the idea, popular for decades in the 20th century, that therapists should simply encourage people to try to remember, and relive, hurtful emotional experiences and that, somehow, by doing that, it would enlighten the patient and bring about beneficial change. We can now see that this approach was unhelpful. Reviving and reliving emotional experiences doesn't change the maps of reality. Instead it tends to strengthen or further distort the inaccurate maps and make things worse. A depressed person gets more depressed; an angry person more angry; an anxious person becomes more anxious. That's why psychodynamic approaches can so often make people worse and keep them in therapy.

Psychodynamic therapists could more productively use their skills by recognising that, when people have a need to understand their past, they must first develop a degree of detachment to enable them to observe the way they have been conditioned. When patients understand the distorted templates they developed in their attempt to structure their lives to survive the inadequacies of their environmental and learning experiences, it becomes easier for them to detach from them and move on. But they can only review and understand their past in this way if, first, they are helped to become less emotional about it. In other words, the therapist has to help the patient go into their 'observing self' in order to develop a dispassionate understanding of their own past. This is, in many ways, the reverse of what happens in most forms of psychodynamic therapy and counselling, where encouraging people to dig into, or recover, their 'memory' and relive earlier emotional experiences merely strengthens those inappropriate metaphors through which the person is miserably experiencing their life in the here and now.

Memory is both a constructive and creative experience and we can't randomly access it. When we access a memory in the present to illustrate a point or solve a problem we do so through metaphor. Our brain automatically goes on a metaphorical search, looking for experiences in the past that will confirm our idea of what we think our problem is about.

This means that any therapist taking a person back into their past is *inevitably* going to come up with metaphorical representations of their current predicament. This, however, doesn't imply that the metaphorical representations are true: it is simply a reflection of how the problem is formulated. Memory has to distort the past in order to get the best metaphorical fit to the idea that's prompting the search. Neither does it imply that those metaphorical analogues of a current dilemma are in fact the origin of that dilemma. Because a memory is largely recreated each time it is recalled, we cannot be sure that the analogous pattern it comes up with is a significant contributor to the presenting problem. And, in any case, once a therapist recognises that a metaphorical template is wrong, it really doesn't matter at what point it is changed, or what specific instance of its existence is changed, so long as the pattern is altered.

The very metaphorical process that creates problems when it goes awry can itself also be used therapeutically to help resolve problems. So, for instance, to help a person with an anxiety disorder, a therapist might use metaphor to give them a model of what they are experiencing that makes their experience understandable and controllable. For example, intense anxiety can be likened to the 'fast spin' of a washing machine. Anxiety is a 'programme' that is activated for a specific purpose, namely to let the person flee from danger. But if the danger doesn't exist, except in their imagination, it is simply like the fast spin on a washing machine being inadvertently switched on while the machine is empty. The therapist can then explain how an anxious person is keeping it switched on by a sort of feedback loop that is falsely indicating that danger continues to exist. The anxiety is maintained through a misinterpretation of what is happening.

Just using that metaphor can, we have found, sufficiently reduce many people's anxiety, and bewilderment, so that their problem goes away.

Metaphor can also be used in the form of a story or anecdote, or a cast of characters that parallels the patient's experience or problem. Then, through the metaphor, the therapist can provide a more helpful way for the client to look at their problem, or offer suggestions as to what to do differently that could help solve it. We might, for instance, tell a story of someone else who had similar problems and how they helped themselves get better.

The right hemisphere of the brain has a natural facility to understand metaphor and, because the pattern of the problem is already represented in the patient's mind, can identify the matching template contained in the story. A story can help people to recognise and really see themselves in a way that no amount of 'factual' information can.[64]

Metaphors are effective in therapy for many other reasons. They build a sense of expectancy in the patient that their own problem too can be resolved. In effect, "the suspending of ordinary constraints helps people to reclaim optimism and to fuel the imagination with energy for the attainment of goals: whether moral or material."[65] They can help a client bypass the natural resistance to change. Because they are stories, metaphors can be used to present directives and suggestions in such a way as to maximise the possibility that they will be accepted. By presenting advice in this way the patient also feels under less pressure to accept the advice.

Metaphors foster clients' independence. It is the clients who have to translate the meaning of the story and decide whether to take action based on this new perspective. They can, as a result, take more credit for the changes that develop. The process also enhances the client's flexibility of thinking since understanding metaphor involves the more creative and intuitive right hemisphere of the brain.

Using metaphors also carries minimum risk. Should the patient feel the advice in the story is not relevant to them, or should they miss the point of the story, little is lost. They feel that they have heard a mildly engaging story and the conversation proceeds without any loss of rapport. Often, though, the meaning of the story may register with them at a later time.

Dream metaphors which clients bring to therapy can also have the therapeutic value of helping them to see objectively what is troubling them emotionally. The dream metaphors can also be useful for helping the therapist realise how the client is really feeling about the therapeutic relationship. Their real feelings can come out in the dreams and metaphors – or songs they may spontaneously burst into, as clients sometimes report doing. Calmly studying one's dreams also strengthens the observing self, as the person steps back and looks dispassionately at the emotional templates expressed in their dreams.

The brain entranced

We could not continue to exist and evolve without having developed the ability to focus our attention. Primitive creatures automatically react to a stimulus in the same way each time they are exposed to it. The more evolved the creature, the more ability it has to choose to focus on certain elements in its surroundings and cut out others. That essentially is what happens in the trance phenomenon. When the emotional brain is aroused in any way, we go into trance. And this is true throughout the animal kingdom. A cat's hunting and hunger emotions, for example, cause it to focus its attention on a mouse hole. This is an instinct driven trance state and the cat is not easily distracted.

All animals, including our ancestors, operated through instinct driven trance states long before mankind developed creativity. When we get emotional about anything, we slip into an instinct driven trance. If we get angry, we are in a trance, totally focused on the 'rightness' of our actions and not open at that moment to considering anything else. We just have the one focus, as do animals. One experiment carried out with dogs involved a wire fence too high for the dogs to jump over, although it was possible for them to run round either side of it. Meat was placed behind the middle of the fence. When the experimenters used dogs that were calm, the dogs easily saw how to get at the meat and ran round the fence. But when they used dogs that were very hungry, those dogs just stayed in front of the meat behind the fence, barking with frustration until they collapsed with exhaustion.[66]

Equally inappropriate are the trance states of depression or anxiety. Therapists need to work upon these inappropriate trance states to help patients learn more appropriate ones, which is why many therapists place such importance on metaphor. They recognise that people are often activating the wrong metaphor, the wrong analogue, the wrong story in their life.[67] This is why sexual instincts sometimes express themselves so strangely. Instead of being fixated on the flesh and blood reality of a woman as an object of desire, for example, a man can become fixated on women's shoes or an item of female clothing or some other experience which he associates with the pattern laid down during his early experiences of intense sexual arousal. The sexual arousal metaphor is not matched accurately enough to the real world.

Trance and the metaphorical matching process are inseparable.

The opposite of the trance state is when we widen our focus of attention and free ourselves from metaphors. That is a state that Milton Erickson calls the 'Therapy Trance State' and which mystics call 'State of No Mind', where you just simply relax and go back into your observing self. And, of course, when you do that, you are free from emotions for a while. To help people, very often they have to be taught how to relax mentally and physically, because, if they can get that balance back in their lives, they can avoid staying stuck in a depressive or anxiety trance. When they gain perspective by pulling back into their observing self they can learn about the metaphorical patterns they are using and whether they are appropriate or not. When they do that they have a choice of different routes through their difficulties.

We have written elsewhere[68] about the importance of pattern matching and the range of ways to introduce new patterns into a patient's life in order that they can make changes.

The future

As therapists become more aware of the human givens one of the great benefits that will immediately flow into their professional lives will be a tremendous sense of freedom.

We now understand why theories of human function become so complex. We now have the insight and the ability to discard the complexity and extract those active ingredients within diverse therapeutic traditions which reflect aspects of the human givens and are of therapeutic value. This will enable us to restructure our therapeutic ability organically and apply it in a way that meets the individual needs of the individual client.

The human givens approach also highlights the fact that therapeutic practice need not be based upon prolonged academic training. The essential skills are human skills and, provided a person has a natural talent for working in this area, the skills can be acquired and learned quite rapidly, particularly if taught in a natural way, with the teachers and trainers *actually demonstrating the skills.*

Of course a background knowledge of how human beings function, derived from studies in psychology, biology and mind-body connections, is also essential for therapists. We should never stop learning. And as we learn more and more about the powers and possibilities of the human organism, it becomes ever clearer that there is no room for closed minds about anything. That is why we feel the human givens approach to therapy is so important. Not only does it have enormous cost saving benefits for the psychotherapy field, but it is an open and evolving concept that frees us to see more clearly what really works and why, and thus empowers us to be more effective when relieving distress.

*

Organising Idea No. 1 – new edition
Hypnosis and Trance States

This is the first fully referenced explanation of hypnosis from an evolutionary perspective. *Hypnosis and Trance States: a new psychobiological explanation* offers scientists, researchers, psychologists, psychotherapists, hypnotherapists and the interested lay public, an explanatory 'organising idea' in order to widen and deepen our understanding of the subject. Furthermore, it resolves the controversy of whether hypnosis is an altered state of consciousness or not.

Organising Idea No. 3 – new edition
Breaking the Cycle of Depression

Containing a major new insight about the psychobiology of depression derived from the human givens perspective, this monograph quickly demolishes the myths that abound in our society about the subject. It sets out a clear explanation of what depression is and how best to lift it (illustrated by case histories showing how easily this can be done – when you know how).

Organising Idea No. 4
The APET model: patterns in the brain

For a long time there has been a need for a new model of psychotherapy that integrates the major scientific findings of recent decades with the best of therapeutic practice from diverse disciplines. The APET model was developed as a result of research findings about the pattern-matching nature of brain functioning and offers a way to realign cognitive behavioural therapy to scientifically incorporate the latest neurophysiological and psychological discoveries into a practical methodology for effective brief counselling.

Organising Idea No. 5
The Shackled Brain

There is a lack of agreement in the medical profession about how best to deal with psychological trauma. Some counselling approaches, such as critical incident debriefing and flooding, often deepen trauma rather than remove it. This monograph, *The Shackled Brain: how to release locked-in patterns of trauma*, gives the first neurobiological explanation for what provokes the symptoms. It also describes in detail the most effective way to treat PTSD, phobia, panic attacks and obsessive compulsive disorder (OCD).

£4.95 each (+£1 each p&p) Cheques payable to 'Human Givens Publishing Ltd'
From: Human Givens Publishing, Chalvington, East Sussex BN27 3TD.
To pay by credit card call: **01323 811662** Or buy online at: **www.humangivens.com**

References

1   Dawe, R. M. (1994). *House of Cards: Psychology and psychotherapy built on myth*. Simon & Schuster.

2   Dineen, T. (1996). *Manufacturing Victims: What the psychology industry is doing to people*. Robert Davies.

3   "Pulling findings from the trials, it seems that patients referred to counsellors felt themselves better understood and listened to and were more likely to declare themselves satisfied with their treatment but there was no actual difference in patients' ways of coping with their difficulties or their knowledge of what needed to be changed in their lives. There was no difference in social adjustment between those who were counselled and those cared for just by GPs." Counselling in primary care: a systematic review of the research evidence. *British Journal of Guidance and Counselling*. (2000), 28, 2, 215-231.

4   Miller, S. D., Hubble M. A., and Duncan B. L. (1995) No more bells and whistles. *Family Therapy Networker*, vol.19, no 2.

5   Robertson, I. (2000) This trembling web: the brain and beyond. *The New Therapist*. Vol 7, 3.

6   The 'human givens' concept was developed as part of a human givens therapy training programme for therapists and counsellors developed by several members of the European Therapy Studies Institute (ETSI). The first formal presentation of the 'human givens' approach was made in a series of seminars on effective anxiety management prepared by ETSI and attended by over 3,000 health workers throughout the UK in 1997. The huge number of enquiries for literature on this approach led to the writing of this monograph.

7   Dewdney, A.K. (1997) *Yes we have No Neutrons – A tour through the twists and turns of bad science*. John Wiley & Sons.

8   Webster, R. (1995) *Why Freud was Wrong*. Harper Collins

9   Julian Jaynes, writing on Behaviourism says, "But the single inherent reason for its success was not its truth, but its programme ... with its promise of reducing all conduct to a handful of reflexes and conditional responses developed from them, and generalising the spinal reflex terminology of stimulus and response and reinforcement to the puzzles of headed behaviour and so seeming to solve them ... In all this there was a heady excitement that is difficult to relate at this remove. Complexity would be made simple, darkness would be made light, and philosophy would be a thing of the past ... off the printed page, behaviourism was only a refusal to talk about consciousness." Nobody really believed he was not conscious, and there was a very real hypocrisy abroad, as those interested in its problems were forcibly excluded from academic psychology."
Jaynes, J. (1976), *The Origin of Consciousness in the Breakdown of the Bicameral Mind*, p.15, Houghton, Mifflin Co. Boston

10 "When I can sensitively understand the feelings which they are expressing, when I am able to accept them as separate persons in their own right, then I find that they tend to move in certain directions. And what are these directions in which they tend to move? The words which I believe are most truly descriptive are words such as positive, constructive, moving towards self-actualization, growing towards maturity, growing towards socialization ... to discover the strongly positive directional tendencies which exist in them, as in all of us, at the deepest levels."
The Carl Rogers Reader (1990), Constable, London p.28
"In Roger's view (1980) what psychologically troubled people most need is not to be analysed, judged or advised, but simply to be heard - that is, to be truly understood and respected by another human being. Therefore the primary effort of client centred therapists is to apply all other powers of attention, intuition and empathy to the task of grasping what the client is actually feeling."
Abnormal Psychology, 5th edition, p.193, McGraw Hill (1988)

11 Yapko, M. (1992) *Hypnosis and the Treatment of Depressions*. Brunner Mazel, New York.

12 Mental health promotion in high risk groups. *Effective Health Care* (1997). vol 3, no 3.

13 The following excerpt from a recent book by psychologist Adrian Wells, one of the more innovative and original contributors to cognitive therapy, shows how easily the language of cognitive therapy becomes impenetrable to an outsider and how the process of complexification of theory continues apace. "Schema theory represents a general framework for exploring and conceptualising cognitive behavioural factors in the maintenance of anxiety. However, for cognitive therapy to evolve and for treatment effectiveness to increase, specific models of cognitive - behavioural factors associated with vulnerability and problem maintenance are required. Specific models based on generic schema theory principles have been advanced for panic disorders (Clark, 1985), social phobia (Clark & Wells, 1995) and obsessional problems (Salkovskis, 1985; Wells and Mathews, 1994). These approaches have attempted to integrate schema theory with other psychological concepts considered to be important in specific disorders. The aim in all of these cases is the construction of a model that can be used for individual case conceptualisation for guiding the focus of interventions, and for generating testable model-based hypotheses. Even when specific models are lacking, case conceptualisation and treatments may be based on operationalising basic constructs of the general theory on a case by case basis."
Wells, A. (1997) *Cognitive Therapy on Anxiety Disorders*, p. 14, John Wiley & Sons, Chichester & New York.

14 Yapko, M. (1992) *Hypnosis and the Treatment of Depressions*. Brunner Mazel, New York.

15 Luborsky, L. and Singer, B. (1975). *Comparative Studies of Psychotherapies: Is it true that "everyone has one and all must have prizes?"* Basic Books, New York.

16 Danton, W, Antonuccio, D. and DeNelsky, G. (1995). Depression: Psychotherapy is the best medicine. *Professional Psychology Research and Practice*, 26, 574.

17 Danton, W., Antonuccio, D. and Rosenthal, Z. (1997). No need to panic. *The Therapist*, vol 4, no 4.

18 Roth, A. Fonagy, P. et al (1996). *What Works for Whom.* The Guildford Press, New York, London.

19 Golman, D. (1996). *Emotional Intelligence.* Bloomsbury Publishing, London.

20 Zilman, D. (1988). Mental control of angry aggression. In Wegner and Pennbaker, *Handbook of Mental Control.* Touchstone, New York.

21 Tyrrell, I. (1997). *Tranceform.* ETSI.

22 Wolinksky, S. (1991). *Trances People Live.* The Bramble Company, Connecticut.

23 Csikszentmihalyi, M. (1992) *Flow: the psychology of happiness,* Harper & Row

24 Griffin, J. (1997). *The Origin of Dreams.* The Therapist Ltd.

25 Shapiro, F (1997). *EMDR.* Basic Books, New York.

26 Griffin, J. (1997) op. cit.

27 Griffin, J. (1997) op. cit.

28 Yapko, M. (1992) *Hypnosis and the treatment of depressions.* Brunner Mazel, New York.

29 Seligman, M. in Levitt, E. Lubin, B. & Brooks, J. (eds), *Depression; Concepts, controversies and some new facts* (2nd ed.) Erlbaum, Hillsdale.

30 Yapko, M. D. (ed) (1989). *Brief Therapy Approaches to Treating Anxiety and Depression.* Brunner/Mazel.

31 Deikman, A J (1982). *The Observing Self.* Beacon Press.

32 Narrative therapy is a form of therapy developed by Michael White and Jacob Epstein which helps patients reinterpret their past experiences in a way that reflects them in a better light so they can perceive themselves as being more empowered and less victims of their history.

33 Griffin, J. and Tyrrell, I. (2001). *The Shackled Brain: How to release locked-in patterns of trauma.* Human Givens Publishing.

34 O'Hanlon, W.H. (1994) *Psychotherapy's Third Wave? The promise of narrative,* Reprinted with permission from The Family Therapy Networker (USA) in The Therapist, Vol 2 No.4

35 White, M. and Epston, D. (1990). *Narrative Means to Therapeutic Ends.* Norton, New York.

36 Suls J. and Mullen B. (1981). Life events, perceived control and illness: the role of uncertainty. *Journal of Human Stress*, 7, 30.

37 Winn, D. (1983) *The Manipulated Mind,* The Octagon Press, London.
38 Erlich, P. and Ornstein, R. (1989) *New World, New Mind.* Doubleday
39 Ornstein R. and Sobel, D. (1988). *The Healing Brain.* Macmillan.
40 Moir, W. and Moir, A. (1998) *Why Men Don't Iron,* Channel Four Books
41 Tannon, D. (1990) *You just don't understand.* William Morrow & Co. Inc., New York.
42 Reilly, J. S. *et al.,* 'Consumer Product Aspiration and Ingestion in Children: Analysis of emergency room reports to the national electronic injury surveillance system', *Annals, Otology, Rhinology and Laryngology* (9 Sept. 1992), Vol.101 (9), 739-41; Kotch, J., 'Child Day Care and Home Injuries Involving Playground Equipment', *Journal Paediatrics Child Health* (June 1993), Vol.29 (3),222-7; Towneer, E.M. L., *et al.,* 'Measuring Exposure to Injury Risk in Schoolchildren Aged 11-14', *British Medical Journal* (12 Feb. 1994), Vol.308, 449; Centres for Disease Control and Prevention, 'Morbidity and Mortality Weekly Report: Youth risk behavior surveillance – United States', *CDC Surveillance Summaries* (27 Sept.1996), Vol.45 (No. SS-4).
43 *Diagnostic and Statistical Manual of Mental Disorders,* 82.
44 Gonen, B., et al., 'The Effects of Short-Term Feeding of a High Carbohydrate Diet on HDL Subclasses in Normal Subjects', *Metabolism* (1981), Vol.30, 1125-9; Knuiman, J. T., et al., 'Total Cholesterol and High Density Lipoprotein Cholesterol Levels in Populations Differing in Fat and Carbohydrate Intake', *Arteriosclerlosis* (1987), Vol.7,612-19; Mensink, R. P., et al., 'Effects of Monounsaturated Fatty Acids Versus Complex Carbo-hydrates on High-Density Lipoproteins in Healthy Men and Women', *Lancet*(1987), 122-5.
45 Shah, I. (1978). *Learning How to Learn.* Octagon Press.
46 Daniel, N. (1975). *The Arabs and Medieval Europe.* London & Beirut.
47 Csikszentmihalyi, M. (1992) op cit.
48 "Don't aim at success – the more you aim at it and make it a target, the more you are going to miss it. For success, like happiness, cannot be pursued; it must ensue ... as the unintended side-effect of one's personal dedication to a course greater than oneself." Frankl, V. (1978) *Man's Unheard Cry for Meaning,* Simon & Schuster, New York
49 Beavers, R. (1990). *Successful Families.* Norton, New York.
50 Ornstein, R. and Sobel, D. (1989). *Healthy Pleasures.* Addison Wesley, New York.
51 Martin, P. (1997). *The Sickening Mind: Brain, behaviour, immunity and disease.* Harper Collins, London.
52 Kotulak, R. (1997). *Inside the Brain.* Andrew McMeel Publishing.
53 McEwen, B. and Stellar, E. (1993). Stress and metastasis. *Archives of Internal Medicine* , 153.

54 Ornstein R. and Thompson, R. (1985). *The Amazing Brain*. Chatto & Windus.
55 Griffin, J (1997) op cit.
56 Griffin, J (1997) op cit.
57 Foulkes, D.(1978) A Grammar of Dreams, New York, Basic Books.
58 Aserinsky, E. & Kleitman, N. (1953). Regularly occurring periods of eye mobility and concomitant phenomena during sleep. *Science*, 118, 273-274.
59 Jouvet, M. & Michel, F. (1959). Correlations Electromyographiques du Sommeil chez le Chat Decortique et Mesencephalique. *Chronique Comptes Rendus de la Societe Biologie*, 154, 422-425.
60 Jouvet, M. (1965). Paradoxical sleep – a study of its nature and mechanisms. *Prog Brain Research*, 18, 20-57.
61 Silveira, R (1994) *Children, Television, fear and violence,* The Therapist, Vol. 2, No 1.
62 Glyn-Jones. A. (1996) *Holding up a Mirror – How Civilizations Decline.* Century.
63 Griffin, J (1997) op cit.
64 Barker, P. (1985). *Using Metaphor in Psychotherapy.* Brunner Mazel, New York.
65 Shah, I. (1979). *World Tales.* Octagon Press, London.
66 Spitz, R. (1965) *The First Year of Life,* International Universities Press, New York.
67 Griffin, J. and Tyrrell, I. (2000). *Breaking the cycle of depression.* Human Givens Publishing.
68 Griffin, J. and Tyrrell, I. (2000). *The APET model: Patterns in the brain.* Human Givens Publishing.

About the authors

JOE GRIFFIN is a psychologist with a thriving psychotherapy practice. Over the last decade thousands of health professionals have enjoyed his practical workshops and seminars on effective psychotherapy and counselling. He is widely recognised as one of the most informed and entertaining speakers on the subject having studied with many of the leading figures of the psychotherapy world. He spent 12 years researching why animals and humans evolved to dream. The resulting book, which describes the breakthrough he made in this field, *The Origin of Dreams,* offered the first holistic synthesis – a recognition of the interdependence of the biological and the psychological – to explain the origin, function and meaning of dreams. His findings about mental processes have been described by scientific reviewers as, "the key to all psychic states ... an important milestone ... moves our understanding on significantly ... a watershed in our exploration of the evolution of mental processes." He is currently working on a new way of understanding evolutionary processes.

IVAN TYRRELL is a psychotherapist (specialising in brief therapy for depression and anxiety disorders) and a writer with a particular interest in the psychology of perception. He is a founder member of the European Therapy Studies Institute (ETSI) which, in 1992, launched *The Therapist* – the popular multi-disciplinary magazine for all caring professionals. His work for *The Therapist* (now called *Human Givens: the mental health journal*) involves him in a continuing programme of writing, interviewing, and investigating the latest developments in psychology, psychotherapy and the study of human behaviour. He lectures at educational and medical institutions throughout the UK. The *British Medical Journal* said of his book, *The Survival Option,* published by Jonathan Cape, "his practical information is reliable", and *The Times* wrote that it contained, "facts, not emotion... should be in every home in the country." Both he and Joe Griffin are members of the group involved with developing the 'human givens' approach to applying knowledge of human psychology and behaviour to psychotherapy, counselling and education.